One Friend?
Two Friends?
Bad Friend?
Good Friend?

By Desiree Panlilio
Encouraging Teens
The teen's guide to creating lifelong friendships

One Friend?
Two Friends?
Bad Friend?
Good Friend?

ENCOURAGING
TEENS — LIFE COACHING

Publisher: Encouraging Teens: https://encouragingteens.com

Project Manager: Renee Bobb, The Book Publishing Lady
Editor: Tracy Johnson Proof Your Point
Book Cover Designer: Joseph Okerentie

Printed in the United States of America
First Edition: July 2022

ISBN Paperback: 979-8-9865763-1-2

Library of Congress Control Number: 2022912860

Dedication

To my wonderful, intelligent, and encouraging husband,
Rick Panlilio, who pushes me to be the best person I can be.
For the days where I wanted to give up and you believed in
my dream and goals, thank you.

To my two daughters, Madeline and Rebecca. Without
you, I would have more time on the beach.

But truly, your wit, chaos, and love bring joy and laughter to my
life every day! Without you both, this book would
have never been written.

You two are the inspiration of Encouraging Teens.

Acknowledgments

I have been blessed with many amazing people in my life. My father, Henry Peter Lauzon, told me to never give up and to always do the right thing, even when you stand alone. I have tried to live up to that. His heritage as a Manitoba Metis and the belief he held in the value of family and friends stand firmly in my own values. To Michele Skelly who pushed me off the ledge and helped me launch my business, I am thankful. I am grateful for the many mentors I have had over the years and, most recently, Cheale Villa and Renee Bobb who have helped me move my goals and dream into reality.

To all our military families I have met and have shared the journey of being a military spouse and the challenges we face with multiple moves and helping our children to integrate into yet another community and school, I love each of you. Each one of you helped to make me a better person.

God has blessed me with a supportive village and that has made all the difference.

Ever since humans have been around, we have all wanted to belong, to have friends. However, are some friends better than others? That is a question each individual needs to ask of their community and friends.

Table of Contents

Prologue

The idea for this book is that the material and exercises are opportunities for the reader to gain insight into who they are, and who they want to be around. Deciding who our friends are and who we want to spend time with is a personal choice. However, as with most things in life, it is often helpful to define who we are and what individuals would complement our own personality and challenge us to be a better version of ourselves. Friends are a set of individuals who do just that.

As you journey through this book, take time to reflect on the exercises and journal your own thoughts. Talk with adults and friends as you discover who will make up your village and encourage you to create the success that you want in your future.

1.

What Is A Friend?

Friends, we all want them. It is human nature that we all want to belong, to be part of a social group, and to be accepted. Our desire to belong goes back to the time of the caveman where survival depended on the group. We were stronger as a group. In the time of the caveman, as a group we worked together for the survival of the tribe. Each member of the tribe played an important part and felt a responsibility to the group and to each individual member.

Today, our immediate family fills some of that role. We are each an important member of our family, and as a family unit we successfully navigate life. However, since we are no longer a tribe chasing down or gathering our food (unless you count a trip to the grocery store), our group dynamics have shifted, but we still desire to belong to a group. We have shifted from a tribe to a system where we have family and friends. So yes, today, we all want to be part of a "tribe" to have others notice us and encourage us and at times carry our hopes and dreams. But making, having, and keeping friends takes work. But before you can learn about the making, having, and keeping of friends it is important for you to define for yourself what a friend is. After you have a clear outline of what a friend is, you can decide what you want in a friend and how best to build that friendship.

The basic definition of a friend is someone who is there for us and whom we're there for in return. Friendships have their ups and downs. Some friendships are formed in the most unlikely of circumstances or with an individual you never realized was that person you would come to depend on. A friendship might start out nicely, but then you realize it is not the friendship that you or the other person are looking for. And then the friendship dissipates.

All these scenarios are normal as you are developing friendships and more importantly developing your own set of values and defining who you are. As you grow and change in your teenage and young adult years, so will your friends. That is all normal and although frustrating and hurtful it is part of the process in defining who you are and what makes a good friend for you.

We generally share some of the same beliefs and values with our friends. So, let's stop here and answer a few questions.

The first stop on the journey of deciding what is a friend for you is to look at your values. Values drive behavior. They are your beliefs regarding specific issues. Values are internal and specific to you, emotional, arguable, and can and should change as we gain knowledge. What you valued ten years ago is not what you value today. What you value is important, so pause and write down five things you value about yourself. What are some examples? You may value loyalty, honesty, knowledge, humor, academics, athletics, and trustworthiness. All of these are attributes that you have and value in yourself. Take a moment to make a list of your values.

1.

2.

3.

4.

5.

Are those the same values you look for in your friends? Do your friends have the same values? Think about your friends and write down what values you observe in them.

1.

2.

3.

4.

5.

_____

_____

_____

_____

_____

_____

_____

Do you have any values that are opposite for you and your friend? An example is your friend is funny and you are not funny. Or is your friend mean to others but you are not? Look at the list and decide if it's okay to have different values. Is it okay to have different values sometimes but not all the time? Write your answers below.

Signs Of A Good Friend

What makes a good friend? That is a difficult question because friends come in all varieties, and what makes a good friend in one situation may not make a great friend in another. What does that look like? If you play a sport, you may have friends on the team you play on. You practice with these girls and hang out with them during the game and when the team travels for games. However, you may also have friends who you enjoy watching movies with or baking cookies with or horseback riding with. This group of friends is different, and you share different interests and information with them. We all have that small group of friends that we share "everything" with, that core group you trust with everything. But stop and take a moment to look at some definitions of what makes a good friend. Here are some signs of a good friend.

1. A good friend will always be there for you, no matter what. They aren't going to run away because you failed a test or because you moved farther away. Friends know that life has many challenges, and they will stick with you through those challenges to the end.

2. A good friend listens and keeps secrets. Build Trust. We will talk about trust by itself. That is a big word.

3. A good friend will be one who you enjoy spending time with.

4. A good friend shows empathy. A friendship where friends are not taking into consideration each other's feelings is not

a good friendship. It is one that either is or will become one sided.

5. A good friend forgives. They do not hold the past against the other friend. They learn from their mistakes and move on. Part of this is giving grace and the other part is building and having trust in the friendship.

What would you add to the list of what makes a good friend? Add your comments below.

_____

_____

_____

_____

_____

_____

_____

_____

_____

_____

_____

_____

3.

Signs Of A Bad Friend

Just as important to ask yourself what a good friend is, you must also decide what a bad friend is. What makes a person a bad friend for you? What are the behaviors or things that a person would do that would make you consider them a bad friend? Stop and look at this list of what may make a bad friend.

1. The User friend. Some so-called friends only want you when they need something.

2. The Trash Talker friend. If your friend is always talking trash about their other friends to you, then don't think you are an exception. Once you are not within earshot, your friend is talking trash about you.

3. The friend who doesn't like criticism. A good friend will take the criticism to heart and realize the criticism is a way to help them grow. A bad friend may feel attacked, become aggressive, and even stop being your friend when you say something they do not want to hear.

4. The friend who doesn't like differences. This is the friend who wants everyone to be the same and do the same thing. This is the mean girl. Is that the type of friend you want?

5. The friend who makes excuses to not hang out with you. If you're the one who is always making plans and they're the

one who never hangs with you despite always saying how much they miss you, they may not be a good friend.

6. The Push friend. You must do what they want. They are trying to "run" your life. They do not want you to have your own life unless it works with their plans.

What would you add to the list of what makes a bad friend? Add your comments below.

_____

_____

_____

_____

_____

_____

_____

_____

_____

_____

_____

_____

_____

It is easy to look back on friendships and decide if a past friend was a good friend or a bad friend. It is also a great opportunity to look at the friendships you are currently in and decide if you are in a bad friendship. Take a moment to reflect on the friendships you enjoy and why you enjoy them. Also, what friendships do you find take a lot of time, emotion, and drama? What friendships do you struggle with? As you learn about yourself, you will also learn about what friendships you want to spend time in and on. Take a moment to journal and reflect on your thoughts.

4.

Trust

Before we begin, please realize that the work starts with you. How often do we say to one of our friends or family members that we trust them? Or we may end a friendship because we no longer trust the individual. Trust is a word we are quick to use, but when we pause and think about it, what does trust mean? Take a moment to answer the following questions as you decide for yourself what the word trust means.

What is trust?

_____

_____

_____

_____

_____

_____

_____

_____

How do you define trust?

_____

_____

_____

_____

_____

What makes you trust one person but not another?

_____

_____

_____

_____

_____

_____

_____

_____

_____

_____

_____

Trust is built in the smallest of moments. It is when your friend stands up for you when you are not around. It is when your parents show up for your game because they said they would be there. Trust is asking for help when you need it and having someone to be there when your words fail you and you are looking to someone else for strength. Trust is all these things and so many more. Trust is an emotion. It is a feeling we have about our friends and family, and we depend on it to keep our friendships intact. After all, if you do not trust someone, are you still friends?

Trust has several parts. We are going to look at the parts of trust and then you will write down how you personalize the belief of trust.

Trust begins with boundaries. Boundaries are what you are willing to ask a friend to do. Also, it is making sure that you would never ask your friend to do something that compromises their values and integrity. That boundary is reciprocated to you as well. It is a part of the friendship where you understand what one another's comfort level is and what you each define as your values and principles that weave our society and community together.

Think about boundaries. Has there been a time when someone asked you to do something that went against your boundary? It could have been a time when your friend used your phone to post something on your social media site, or it could have been a time when your friend borrowed your clothes without asking.

Has a friend ever pushed your boundary? How did you feel?

_____

_____

_____

_____

_____

What could you say or do when a friend pushes against one of your boundaries?

_____

_____

_____

_____

_____

Another part of trust is reliability. You do what you say you will do. That makes us trust our friends. As well, your friend does what they say they will do. If your friend told you that they would meet you after school, and then they did, that is being reliable. It is important to be reliable to do what you say you are going to do.

Has there been a time when you have not been reliable? How did you feel?

_____

_____

_____

_____

_____

_____

_____

Was there a time when a friend was not reliable? How did you feel?

_____

_____

_____

_____

_____

What could you say or do when a friend is not reliable? Is that fair?

_____

_____

_____

_____

_____

Trust also requires accountability and honesty. Accountability is being responsible for your choices and having your friend being accountable for their choices. This blends with honesty as it means telling the truth, and sometimes that is hard. At times it may seem easier to not be accountable and not be honest with a friend or parent. However, that ends with more frustration, anger, and a breakdown in trust and the friendship. An example may be not telling your friend the truth why you canceled plans with them. Or it may be that you participated in the gossip about your friend and now you need to be responsible and hold yourself accountable. Being accountable and honest are hard and uncomfortable.

Has there been a time when you were not honest or accountable for your choices with a friend? How did you feel?

_____

_____

_____

_____

_____

_____

Was there a time when your friend was dishonest or did not accept responsibility or accountability for their choice? How did you feel?

_____

_____

_____

_____

_____

_____

What could you say or do when your friend is not accountable or honest? Are there certain things you could not forgive your friend for if they were not honest about the choice from the start?

_____

_____

_____

_____

_____

_____

_____

Just as accountability and honesty are part of trust, so is generosity and Grace. What do generosity and grace have to do with trust? In a friendship we want to be generous toward our friends. It is assuming the most generous thing about your friend. It is believing that they would not say something mean or gossip about you. It is then having the grace to check in with them about what you have heard. Being generous is about believing the best in your friend and the grace to not say something different to people about your friend.

This all centers around gossip and how everyone likes to hear gossip until it is about them, then it is a different feeling and the thought creeps in to be mean and add to the gossip. This is where generosity and grace come into play. It is one of the hardest attributes of trust. It is often hard to stand firm in your trust of your friend and be both generous and give them grace when you are hearing rumors of things they may have shared about you. Here's another example of grace. If your friend is late to meet you, you can believe that they did not mean to be late, that it was only a series of events that made them delayed.

Just as you give your friend generosity and grace, so should your friend do the same with you. It is about checking in and validating gossip or waiting to hear why your friend is late to meet you. It is the generosity in believing your friend only wants the best for you.

Was there a time when you did not give generosity or grace to a friend? How did that feel?

_____

_____

_____

_____

_____

Was there a time when your friend did not give you generosity and grace? How did that change the friendship?

_____

_____

_____

_____

_____

What could you say or do when you forget to give your friend generosity or grace? What if your friend forgot to give you grace and generosity?

_____

_____

_____

_____

_____

_____

Keeping a friend's secret is the cornerstone of trust. Sharing secrets with others can play a big part in breaking trust and ending friendships or damaging relationships. When you or your friend share a confidence, that secret should not be shared with anyone else.

As well, if you share with your friend someone else's confidence or secret, how can that friend trust to share their confidence with you? A secret told to you is told to you and not yours to share at any time or in any situation. Have you ever had this thought when someone is sharing something they should not? *How can I trust you with my secret?* If you haven't, has this just sparked that thought? If you are sharing someone's secret, can you really be trusted? If your friend is sharing a secret someone told them, can you really share your secrets with this friend?

Have you ever shared a secret someone told you? How did you feel? Was it the right thing to do?

_____

_____

_____

_____

_____

What can you do if you share a secret?

_____

_____

_____

_____

_____

Have you ever had a friend share your secret?
How did you feel?

_____

_____

_____

_____

_____

What can you do if your friend shares your secret?

_____

_____

_____

_____

_____

Trust is an emotional word that we each define in our own way. What would you add to your definition of trust?

_____

_____

_____

_____

_____

_____

_____

_____

_____

5

What Is A Good Friend?

Good friends make you feel good about yourself. A good friend is genuine, someone you can be yourself around. This friend will encourage you unconditionally and accept you as you are. A good friend will also help you to grow and at times tell you uncomfortable truths about yourself to help you achieve the best version of yourself. In turn, if you are a good friend, you do all of this for someone else. Specifically, what are some words you may use to describe a good friend? We touched on trust which is a large component of friendship and relationships, but what other words, traits, and characteristics are required to be or to find a good friend?

In regard to honesty, when things come up in life that may not have been the best choice or if you do something that you regret, you must be able to tell your friend about it. In return, your friend must be able to share those truths with you. Honesty is a part of trust but also is a trait we often vocalize as being important in friendships.

Support is a part of friendship. It is supporting your friend, from being at the opening of the school play to cheering them on at a home game. It is about helping your friend and them helping you. Supporting one another helps to grow the relationship. Support in a larger circle creates a friend group and a sense of community and belonging to the group.

Being a good listener is important for friendship and a quality that makes a good friend. Sometimes we don't need to hear advice. We need someone who will really listen to us—an active listener who is there to pay very close attention to what we choose to tell them. As we talk through issues or feelings, we may come to our own realizations about what has been said. We don't always need to hear someone else's take on what has happened.

A good friend offers comfort. Sometimes we do not want anyone to say anything to us or do anything for us; just the presence of a good friend is all that matters. A good friend is like a big cozy blanket that you wrap around yourself to feel comfortable and protected. When your friend fails a test, they probably don't need any words from you. If your friend has a fight with their parents, all that is needed from you is to be present and offer your silent strength.

Now let's talk about laughter. We all want someone to share jokes with, to let our guard down with. Those moments of inside jokes and shared laughter are often the moments you will remember when you need strength in a difficult or frustrating situation. The moments of laughter help you realize that life is fun and that laughter is an important part of living.

A good friend is a companion. Life is more fun with them. It is often more enjoyable to share trips, hobbies, celebrations, and activities—all the good stuff of life—with someone else. Friends and family are an important part of companionship and making life more fun.

What other words would you use to describe what a good friend is? What do you look for in your friends?

6.

Challenging Friends

As if school was not challenging enough. The academics, the fact that everyone is changing, your friends are changing, you are changing, and now you have challenging friends. What are challenging friends? They are the friends who you often try to avoid or block on social media. However, are there a few warning signs you could be on the lookout for that may help you recognize a challenging personality? If so, you may be able to avoid getting caught up in the behavior, drama, and hurt feelings of yourself and others that these challenging friends seem to be masterful at. The answer is yes, and being able to understand and identify challenging individuals and friends is important to help you manage and distance yourself from these people.

What are some of the signs of a challenging friend?

1.   Have a preoccupation with blaming others, with extreme behavior such as spreading rumors, yelling, or even lying.

2.   The all or nothing approach. In the text message if you are the target, you may read, "this is all your fault," "you are to blame," and/or "I did nothing wrong." Any of those text messages or words sound familiar?

3.   The emotion of the situation does not correlate. In other words, the anger is extreme and nothing can talk them down. In fact, when you respond, the situation escalates and you find yourself trapped in a spiral of blame,

accusations, gossip, and blocking on social media.

4.   Minor problems become huge disputes. For example, showing up late or canceling plans with this friend becomes a huge fight where an apology is not acceptable, and this friend will bring up past fights. They thrive on drama. They do not want a reasonable solution, only their solution.

5.   This person cannot control and cannot solve the problem, and usually the friendship suffers or is ended. They may share everything that is "wrong" with you and how you should behave. They take no responsibility for the friendship.

Challenging friends also have a pattern of behavior you may see. Here are a few examples of the behavior of a challenging friend.

1.   They honestly view other people (perhaps you) as causing the way they feel and the way they act. They may say, "____ makes me feel this way" or "He made me do it." They lie or try to manipulate you.

2.   They do not understand or accept that their own behavior tends to create or worsen situations.

3.   They do not learn from their mistakes but easily repeat them because they are blaming others for their situation.

How do you help a challenging friend? What if the answer is that it is not your responsibility to help the challenging friend? You can certainly suggest that perhaps talking with a school counselor may be beneficial. The best thing you can do is to remove yourself from the challenging friend's influence.

A challenging friend is not a good friend. Take a moment to

review your values and ask yourself what you feel makes a good friend. What are you looking for in a good friend? Now examine the criteria looking through it with the lens of the challenging friend. Chances are your challenging friend does not meet the criteria of being a good friend. Remember, it is not your responsibility to change anyone. You are responsible to yourself and your behavior, and not being influenced by a challenging friend is part of your responsibility.

An important skill to learn is how to remove yourself from a challenging friend's influence. Ending a friendship is a difficult decision, but the process does not have to be. A friendship that does not align with your values must be examined and evaluated to determine what the next step is in the friendship. When you engage in any interaction with a challenging friend you are empowering and supporting that friend and being drawn into their drama and their control. This may have a negative outcome for you as you become their target or become part of what others may feel is the problem.

You may feel you are helping if you say, "Let me tell you what is wrong with you" or use the "Take a look in the mirror, buddy" approach. This is not helpful and will only escalate the problem. The conversation will end abruptly and you will feel frustrated, hurt, and bewildered. Instead, it is best to exit a conversation with a challenging friend and to end the friendship. How can you do that?

It is responding in a friendly but firm tone that provides valid information and does not allow for an argument or an escalation of a situation. The best way to do this is to look at a few examples.

Example one

Carol texts Sharon the following:

Who do you think you are? You're making me look bad!!!! You know you were supposed to help me get my homework done, but noooo. You're so important you thought you could just ignore my text to let me copy the assignment. I couldn't get it done and it's YOUR fault! You need to get your s**t together! You did this last week also and I got a zero. This is a you problem and you better fix it. You are so stuck up.

How would you handle this?

_____

_____

_____

_____

This could spiral out of control quickly, but Sharon understands that Carol is a challenging friend. While Sharon is trying to end the friendship, Carol seems determined to pull Sharon back in.

Here is Sharon's response.

Hey Carol, as I texted last week, I will not let anyone copy my homework assignments. I can, though, make time to help you with the homework. How about Tuesday after school or Saturday morning? The other option is for you to reach out to the teacher for help. Let me know by 11:00 a.m. tomorrow what day and time would work for you. If I don't hear from you by then, I'll just assume you don't need my help.

Here, Sharon provides clear boundaries. Cheating is a boundary, and she lets Carol know that she has asked too much and that it is not part of Sharon's values. The options Sharon is willing to offer are clearly outlined. This takes courage, but Carol is a challenging friend—not a good friend—as she asked Sharon to do something she was uncomfortable with.

Example two

Here is an exchange between Brianna and Sarah.

Brianna: "Hey Sarah, have you heard about Candice?"

Sarah: "Hi Brianna, no I have not heard about Candice, and I am sure if I am meant to know, Candice will share the information with me."

How would you respond?

_____

_____

_____

_____

_____

_____

Sarah, who is Candice's friend, has demonstrated her generosity and grace for Candice who is not present. Sarah refused to hear the gossip and put her good friend's trust and integrity above being pulled into the gossip and rumors about Candice. This takes time and practice but is an essential skill when building friendships and dealing with challenging friends or individuals.

Example three

Now it is your turn. Here is a biology group text.

Brianna: Does anybody know if our biology ecosystem

project is due on Friday or Monday? Mr. Boyd was not clear, and I am so confused.

Jason: I don't know, probably Monday. I am turning it in on Monday. But more important, can you believe Candice got an A? She probably cheated. She is so stuck up and rude to everyone. She is not that smart.

Sarah: Brianna, you are such an idiot! Mr. Boyd has said that it is due Monday. Listen for once. Jason, what is your problem with Candice? Oh, you are just jealous and mad that she wouldn't go on a date with you.

Since you are also part of this group text, what would you do and why?

_____

_____

_____

_____

_____

_____

Think of a personal situation where you were confronted by a challenging friend or part of a group where the situation was challenging. Reflect on that circumstance. How did you handle the situation? How has learning about who a good friend is and your values helped you re-evaluate and look at it differently?

7.

Peer Pressure

What would school be without peer pressure? Well, it would be far easier to navigate and perhaps you would have less acne, get more sleep, and the teen years would be easier. However, there is both positive and negative peer pressure. There's nothing better than having your group of friends and nothing worse than being an outcast. However, as a teen you will experience it all: the awesome close group, the outcast, and everything in between. So, yes, friends are great but never make them your center. Friends as teens can be fickle, talk behind your back, throw you under the bus, have mood swings, and swing back again. Friends move on, pivot, and change friend groups.

As a teenager you are changing, your friends are changing, and your values and goals are maturing and changing. Are your friends congruent with your values, mission statement, and goals? It is okay that your friends change and grow. It is just as important that you change and grow throughout your school career. After all, you are not the same person in third grade as you are now, and you will be a different person when you are twenty. Growth and change are part of the developmental period you are in. But first define peer pressure. Take a moment and write down what you think peer pressure is.

Peer pressure can be both negative and positive. Think of yourself; are you a positive or a negative peer and why? Can you be both?

_____

_____

_____

_____

_____

_____

_____

The definition of peer pressure is rather wordy. Peer pressure is a feeling that you must do the same things as other people of your age and social group in order to be liked or respected by them. What does that mean? It means that you will do certain things to belong to a group. Sometimes those things are good and sometimes not.

Positive peer pressure can benefit your life for the better. It involves encouragement and support rather than actual pressure or persuasion. The group raises you up. It encourages you to achieve your goals and stay true to yourself and your values. Positive peer pressure is seen in study groups, athletic teams, and volunteer groups. Being a member of a positive peer group allows you to avoid the negative peer pressure and being involved in the groups that may not align with your values, goals, and personal mission statement. Being a member of a positive peer group does not mean that the group is always being positive and supportive. Positive peer groups can make fun of a person as well as say discouraging and mean things to another person of the group. It takes knowing what is appropriate and uplifting to another person in the group. It is understanding boundaries and values that the group encourages and then adhering to these guidelines. After all, no one wants to be in a study group where they make fun of a question you ask or ridicule the grade you get on a test. This is true of an athletic team where it is encouraged that you win or lose as a team, and no one is called out or put down for their performance. The critique of your peer group can come from teachers and coaches. As a peer group you want to encourage and empower.

What are ways you can make sure you are a positive peer?

_____

_____

_____

_____

_____

_____

It's just as important to know and understand what a negative peer group could be. You may give in to peer pressure because you want to fit in, be liked, or because you are curious and want to try what others are doing. As a teen you recognize that this is not the best idea, but you also worry about how you will be treated if you don't go along with the group. If you have experienced any of those feelings or encouraged someone to go along with something and you knew it was against their values or crossed their boundaries, that is negative peer pressure. It has a way of creating negative consequences. It is hard to not give into negative peer pressure as a teen because you want to fit in and to be part of that friend group. It is a challenge to find support or the courage to leave a negative peer group. Think about this:

Have you ever been a part of a negative peer group?

_____

_____

_____

_____

_____

How did you feel being part of that group?

_____

_____

_____

_____

How can you make sure you do not get involved in another negative peer group? Who is a resource you can talk to about your concerns and creating and maintaining your boundaries?

_____

_____

_____

_____

8.

Boundaries

Friendships require boundaries. How often have you heard an adult tell you to set boundaries? You think that is great but might ask: What is a boundary and, more importantly, how do I set one or many? Boundaries are limits you establish in order to protect yourself from being hurt, manipulated, or taken advantage of. Boundaries are also an expression of you, what you value, and how you want to be treated. As a teen you are still discovering who you are, but you certainly have a clear idea how you want to be treated and what values you hold fast to. The tough part is sharing your values and not being scared that you will lose out or that your friends will no longer be your friends. Here are three ways to begin setting boundaries.

First, trust your gut. If it feels wrong or you know it is wrong to do something, then speak up or leave. It is the first way to know that what someone is asking of you is wrong and goes against what you value and believe in. You need to be true to who you are, and that is difficult sometimes when you want to be part of a certain group.

Have you ever felt that gut instinct and what did you do?

_____

_____

_____

_____

Second, learn to recognize your feelings in a situation. Are you angry, frustrated, hurt, happy, nervous? Your feelings help you to identify when someone is pushing you to do something that you do not believe in. After all, being angry because someone is asking to copy your homework is a way of knowing that your friend has crossed a boundary and is asking you to do something that is not right.

Third, it is important to respect your friends' boundaries. Friendships are built on respect, trust, and honest communication. Do not ask your friend to do something that you know is in conflict with their values. The example above can easily be reversed. You should not ask your friend to help you cheat on a test because you know it is wrong and steps over the boundary your friend has. Not respecting your friend's boundary will cause the friendship to struggle and may even end the friendship.

The last way to help you establish boundaries is to create some key phrases that can help you buy time and, in the moment, will stop you from making a bad decision in a chaotic moment filled with emotion. Putting these phrases in your phone under notes will allow you to discreetly pull them up in the moment and say the phrase without being pushed into making a bad decision. What are some of these phrases?

1. Let me think about that and get back to you. This phrase allows you the opportunity to not answer and to find a way to make sure that your boundaries are kept and that you are not taken advantage of or manipulated. It allows you to evaluate the ask and maintain your values.

2. No. Yes, that is a complete sentence and you do not need to follow it up with anything. This lets your friend know that they have crossed a boundary and that you are not willing to be a part of whatever it is they have asked you to do. This is a difficult word to say, and it is hard to say no. The fear is that

the friendship will end, but are they really your friend if they ask you to do something that you are strongly opposed to?

3. Let me talk to my parents and let you know. This is another tough phrase to say. Who wants to seem that they need their parent's permission to do anything? That may be what your friend tries to manipulate you with. Your friend may try to push you to do something and make fun of you that you need to check with your parents. However, know that this sentence is powerful and eventually your friend will back down.

4. I am not comfortable doing that or I am not comfortable with that. Can you think of a time when you felt uncomfortable being asked to do something? It is an awkward feeling and one you may dismiss. But don't embrace that gut feeling and emotion. Go ahead and share that you are not comfortable doing what you are being asked and end the conversation. This sentence makes sure that you are not being manipulated. You are also protecting yourself from being hurt or facing consequences that you were aware of before you agreed to do the activity.

Self-Reflections

Self-Reflections

Self-Reflections

Self-Reflections

Self-Reflections

Self-Reflections

Self-Reflections

Self-Reflections

Self-Reflections

Self-Reflections

Self-Reflections

9.

Conclusion

Friendships, particularly teenage friendships, are in a constant state of chaos. The groups are dynamically changing, and you as a teen are dynamically changing and trying to decide where you fit in and where they want to fit in. All of this creates angst and concern for you because you want to belong. We all want to feel loved, to be appreciated, and to be a part of something. As a teen you are also gaining critical thinking skills, metacognition capabilities, and experiencing huge growth physiologically and psychologically.

Wow. I know that is a lot for you to process and you want to create success in your friendship world. I hope this workbook has helped with just that. By understanding who you are, what you are looking for in a friend, and how to build and grow friendships you will create lasting relationships for both your school years and your entire life. Friendships take time, attention, and trust.

About the Author

Desiree Panlilio is the founder and CEO of Encouraging Teens, a Florida-based company that is dedicated to changing and improving the relationships between teens and their parents, their communities, and their peers as they plan for the next steps toward their future.

www.ingramcontent.com/pod-product-compliance
Lightning Source LLC
LaVergne TN
LVHW051210080426
835512LV00019B/3191